Starting Points edited by Henry Pluckrose

Let's
a Pi

Rita Davies

Evans Brothers Limited London

Read this first

Look around you, at home or at school and you will find all kinds of things for making pictures: everyday things which your mother usually throws away, like empty egg boxes, corrugated card and paper, old magazines, milk bottle tops, and many others.

You could begin saving interesting things in a large cardboard box, perhaps at the beginning of a school holiday (you may need to promise to use every article or throw them away when school begins!).

As well as junk material you will need some firm paper or card for many of the pictures, as well as some strong P.V.A. glue which can be bought at any good newsagent or art shop. Glue can be applied with pieces of stiff card or stick. If you already have good paint brushes, don't use these for glue unless you keep them standing in water when in use, and thoroughly wash them afterwards.

Collage pictures—or pictures made with different papers and materials—can be fun to do and many of them look most effective when finally

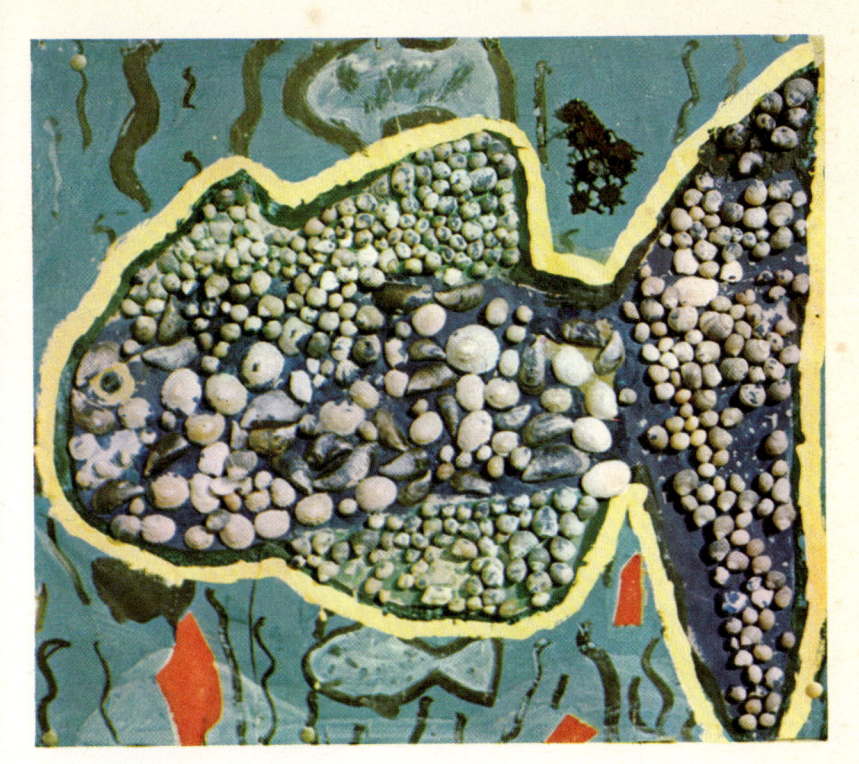

A fish made of shells and stones.

painted. Gold and silver spray—which is easily obtained at Christmas—gives an effective metallic finish to egg box or cardboard pictures.

As with all picture-making, it is advisable to cover yourself before you begin and protect your clothing from sticky glues which may be difficult to remove. One of Dad's old shirts is good for this.

Straw pictures

Collect together
1. Drinking straws
2. Clear glue or paste
3. Black paper
4. Scissors
5. An old brush, or a piece of cardboard for applying glue

How to start
1. Brush one side of the straw with glue.
2. Mount the straws on the black paper, cutting them where necessary.
3. Subjects such as 'A traffic jam', 'The rush hour', 'A building site', all make interesting straw pictures.

Now experiment
You could use paint with your picture by squeezing colour between the straw supports and smoothing it out. Make sure the straws remain clean around the edge.

You might like to paint a background first.

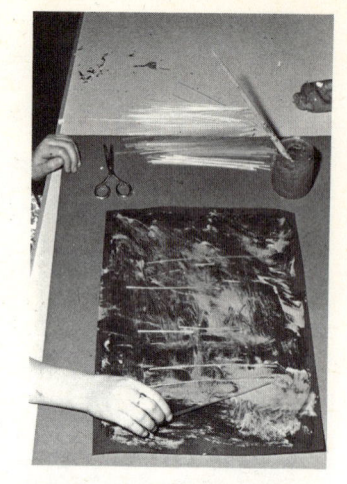

Mounting the straws . . .

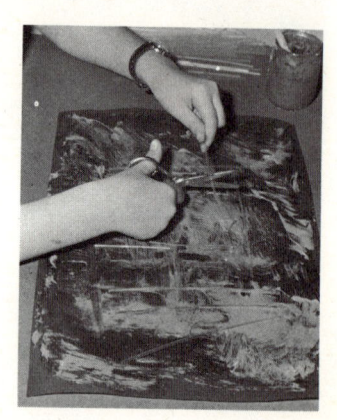

. . . and cutting one to size.

The finished picture.

Silhouette pictures

A silhouette shape is really a shadow, the shape being the most important thing.

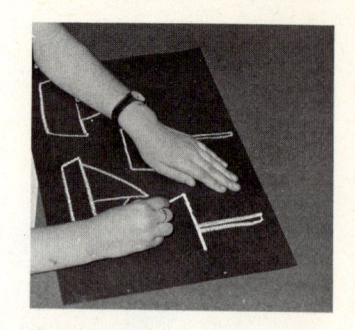

Collect together
1. White paper for mounting
2. Black pastel paper
3. Paste
4. Scissors
5. White pencil or chalk
6. White paint and a brush

Draw the shapes on black paper . . .

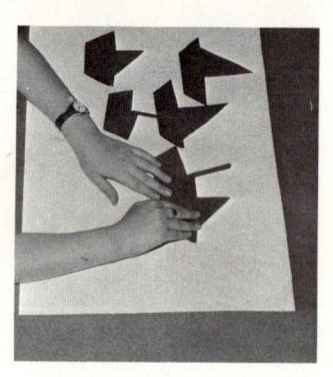

How to start
1. Draw shadow shapes for a picture in pencil or chalk on the black paper. Ships, cars, houses, trees, animals, are all interesting shapes.
2. Cut out the shapes carefully.
3. Group the shapes on the white paper, moving them around until you make a pleasing picture.
4. Stick them with clear paste, on to the white paper.
5. Details can be painted in white on the silhouettes if needed.

. . . and then cut them out and group them.

Now experiment
Give the background paper a colour wash for sky or sea or landscape. Then leave to dry thoroughly before sticking on the silhouettes. A sunset

The boat shapes made an interesting seascape.

sky over the sea with dark boats on it would look effective, or a witch scene, or a picture looking over rooftops— the details of light being added later.

Mosaic pictures

Collect together
1. Sugar paper for mounting
2. Coloured sticky paper
3. Scissors
4. Pencil or crayon

How to start
1. Draw a simple picture or pattern on the sugar paper.
2. Cut the coloured sticky paper into $\frac{1}{2}$ inch squares.
3. Fill the design with these squares, mounting them in straight lines or gentle sweeps or curves. A small gap should be left between each piece to let the sugar paper show through.

Now experiment
You can make mosaic patterns with many different materials—egg shells, broken crockery, rice, seeds, fabric, metal bottle-tops, corrugated card, polystyrene, buttons, etc.

Sticky paper mosaic is useful for decorations at Christmas or Easter, particularly if you use shiny foil paper.

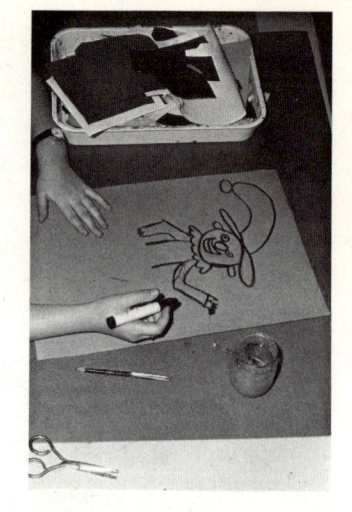

First draw the picture . . .

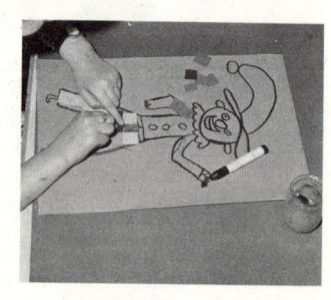

. . . then fill in the shape with sticky paper.

The result is a picture of Mr. Punch.

9

Pictures from tissue paper

Collect together
1. Tissue or crepe paper
2. White paper for mounting
3. Clear paste
4. Scissors
5. A brush

How to start
1. Cut a number of shapes from the tissue (circles, squares, triangles).
2. Paste on to the white paper, touching and overlapping the other shapes so that the colours blend.

Cutting and arranging the shapes.

Now experiment
Make a pattern from circles or squares and limit your colour scheme to two or three colours.

With some friends, look at some paintings by the artist Mondrian for ideas to make up your shapes.

You could use this idea to make a group picture.

The picture shows how the colours blend.

Using torn newspaper

Collect together
1. Dark paper for mounting
2. Newspaper
3. Paste
4. A brush
5. Crayon, oil pastel, or felt pen
6. White chalk

How to start
1. Draw a simple animal or figure shape on the dark paper using white chalk.
2. Fill in the drawing with small torn pieces of newspaper pasted so that no background paper shows through.
3. When the picture is complete draw in the details with pastel, crayon or pen.

Now experiment
Make a picture without sketching any outlines. Subjects such as 'Playing football', 'Playing in the park', are useful titles for pictures made by this method.

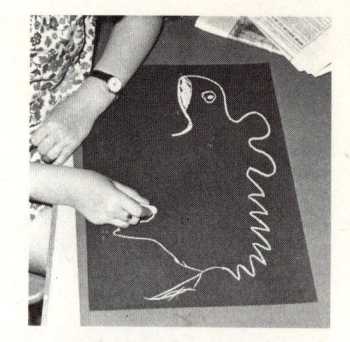

A simple shape is best.

The newspaper must be torn into *small* pieces.

Colour was added to make a fantastic animal.

Making black and white designs

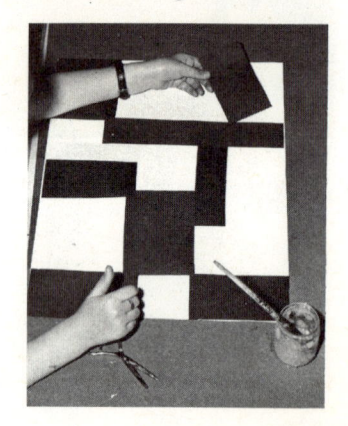

Collect together
1. A sheet of black and a sheet of white paper
2. Scissors
3. Glue
4. An old brush or piece of stiff card for applying glue.

How to start
1. Cut out shapes with straight edges from the piece of black paper.
2. Arrange them on the white sheet so that each piece is touching at some point.
3. Glue the pieces to the white paper. The finished design should look as if it could be white shapes on black paper, as well as black shapes on white paper.

Experiment with your arrangements.

Now experiment
There are many experiments you can make with design, pattern and shapes. You could use two different colours—yellow and black, red and blue, etc. Begin with a black square, cutting and pulling shapes from it and gluing them down on a sheet of white paper.

Make different designs, sometimes using one shape and various colours, or one colour with different shapes.

Here is one sort of arrangement. Is this black on white or white on black?

Using magazines

Collect together
1. Magazines with coloured pages
2. Sugar paper for mounting
3. Paste
4. Brush
5. Scissors
6. White chalk

How to start
1. Draw a simple outline on the sugar paper—an animal, portrait, or picture with large shapes in it.
2. Use the colours in the magazine as if they were your paints, tearing off small pieces of the magazine to paste on to the design.

Now experiment
Make a series of patterned pictures using shades of one colour—for example, find as many different greens as you can. Add tissue paper, sticky paper, etc., or even bits of material. Notice the different textures, patterns and colours. You can work on your finished pictures with chalk, pastel or ink to bring out the detail.

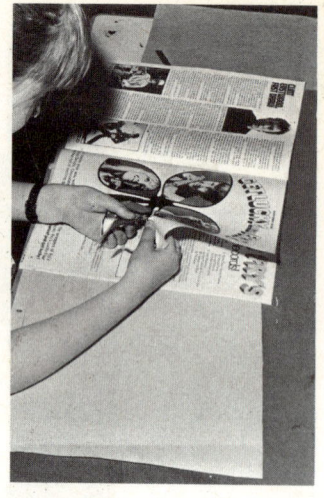

From torn magazine illustrations . . .

. . . you can make an attractive picture.

Ink sprayed pictures

This can be rather messy, so do cover the floor around you with plenty of old newspaper.

Collect together
1. Coloured inks
2. Spray diffusers (or small empty plastic bottles used for hair spray, etc., which can be bought cheaply at chemist shops or chain stores)
3. A piece of sugar or kitchen paper
4. A piece of cardboard
5. Drawing pins
6. An easel or sloped board
7. Scissors

How to start
1. Clip the sugar or kitchen paper on to the easel.
2. Cut out shapes for the picture or design from the cardboard.
3. Pin these on to the sugar paper.
4. Spray the coloured inks from a distance of about 18 inches on to the paper, by blowing through the diffuser or squeezing the bottles.
5. Move the diffuser or bottle to ensure that the colour is a gentle spray and not a series of wet blobs.
6. When dry, remove the shapes.

Cut the shapes . . .

. . . and pin them in position.

Blowing the paint is fun and the result can be very interesting.

Making stencil pictures

Collect together
1. Stencil brush
2. Knife
3. Pencil
4. Sugar paper
5. Stencil paper or thin card (6 inches by 6 inches)
6. Powder paint
7. Scissors

How to start
1. Draw a simple design on a small square of stencil paper or card.
2. Cut this out carefully so as *not* to break the square.
3. Place the square on the sugar paper and use the stencil brush to put on the colour *inside* the cut-out shape.
4. Take off the square carefully and repeat (or use another stencil) making an overall pattern on the paper.

Draw the design . . .

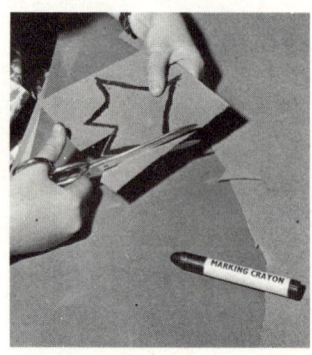

. . . cut it out . . .

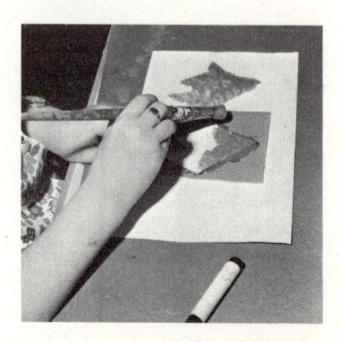

. . . and paint inside the cut-out shape.

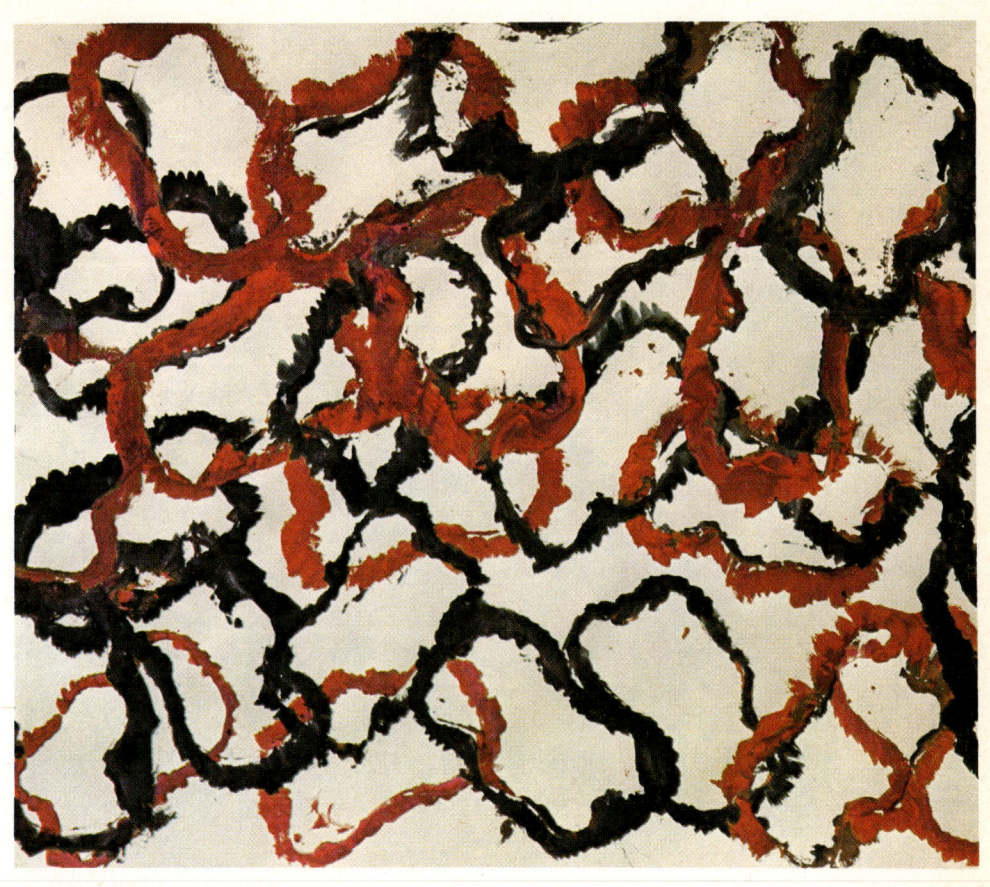

All kinds of patterns can be made. This is
an edge stencil, using the cut-out shape and
painting round the edges only.

Pastel or chalk pictures

Collect together
1. Jar of water
2. Sponge or large brush
3. Some coloured chalks or pastels (not oil, but the hard chalk pastels)
4. Kitchen paper
5. Fixative spray

How to start
There are two methods for making these pictures. In the first method (**A**) the paper is dampened before working, and in the second (**B**) the pastels are dipped in water and used.

A
1. Wet the paper with the sponge.
2. Make sweeping movements across the paper, using the edge of the chalk. Work quickly before the paper dries.

B
You may find this second method easier as you need not worry about the paper drying.
1. Dip your chalk or pastel into the water and use until dry.
2. Make patterns with sweeping movements or by using the thin end of the chalk.

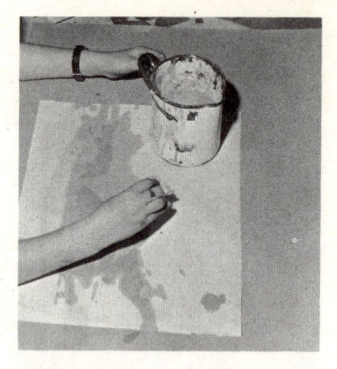

You can use dry chalk on wet paper . . .

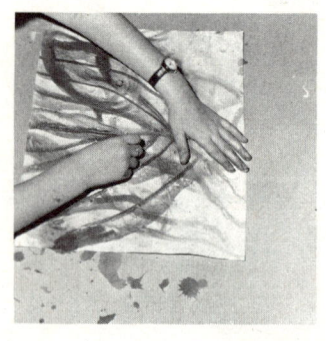

. . . or wet chalk or pastel on dry paper.

A 'still-life' picture in chalk.

Now experiment
It is easier to work with chalks and pastels when they are wet, but your final picture will need fixing so that it does not rub or smudge. Fixative liquid can be obtained in aerosol containers. Spray about 8 inches from the paper.

Pictures on fabric

Collect together
1. A piece of old white sheeting (sacking, hessian or leather can be used when you have practised on the sheeting)
2. Fabric scraps (light and colourful)
3. Glue (cold water paste or Polycell will work, but a stronger P.V.A. adhesive is ideal)
4. Brush
5. Black crayon
6. Scissors

How to start
1. Use the sheeting as a background.
2. Draw a design, a large person or an animal, in black crayon.
3. Fill in the design by cutting small pieces of coloured material and sticking them on to the sheeting.

Now experiment
If you enjoy sewing, you could decorate your final picture with small running stitches—e.g. a clown could have a decorated collar, or a garden scene with flowers would look attractive with stitches to show the details.

Use hessian or stiff plain material as a background and, instead of drawing on

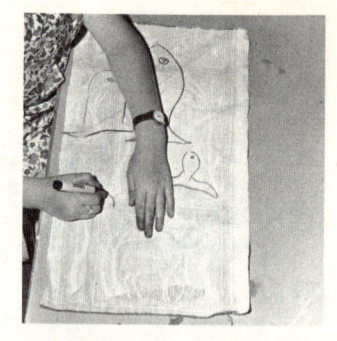

Draw the design on the background material

... and arrange the fabric shapes.

An underwater scene in fabric.

this, use pieces of felt and cut out your shapes directly from these. It may help to make newspaper patterns first. For example, for a picture called 'Animals in the zoo (or jungle)' you could draw and cut out the animals in paper, pin them on felt (or other material scraps), cut them out and place them on the background cloth.

Junk pictures

Collect together
1. A variety of interesting boxes, and discarded or seemingly useless objects (such as tin lids, pieces of string, milk bottle tops, cotton reels, corks, lolly sticks, match-sticks and matchboxes)
2. Strong glue
3. Brush
4. Thickly mixed powder colour (or aerosol tin of paint—e.g. gold or silver or coloured enamel paint)
5. Large sheet of card

All kinds of junk can be used . . .

How to start
1. Collect together a number of interesting objects.
2. Make an abstract design with them or organize them into a picture of a robot, a fantastic machine, or a city of the future.
3. Glue down the pieces.
4. Paint your picture or pin it up and spray it.

. . . to good effect.

Now experiment
Gold or silver colour is very effective for a robot and gives a mechanical appearance. Hold the spray about 8 inches away and move it smoothly so that the paint does not clog or run down the card. If you are using paint, you may want to make a coloured background on your card before starting your picture.

Using material scraps

Collect together
1. Scraps of material—(patterned dress or curtain material, pieces of felt, carpeting, fur, leather, or lace)
2. Glue and brush
3. Pencil
4. Sugar paper or stiff card
5. Scissors

How to start
1. Draw on the sugar paper a design or an outline of a person or an animal (real or fantastic and make-believe).
2. Choose the appropriate material for your picture (e.g. fur for a polar bear, gay cotton or lace for a clown).
3. Cut up small pieces of the material and glue them into place. You may want a mosaic appearance all over, or, in some cases, a larger piece of material would look better. This would apply in a picture of a king, queen, Georgian lady or gentleman, when you could stick on some material for a dress or cloak and work on top with lace, or add buttons, sequins, string or cotton.

Fur fabric . . .

Now experiment
Sometimes a combination of material, paint and crayon is a good idea. Make a background by applying paint with a

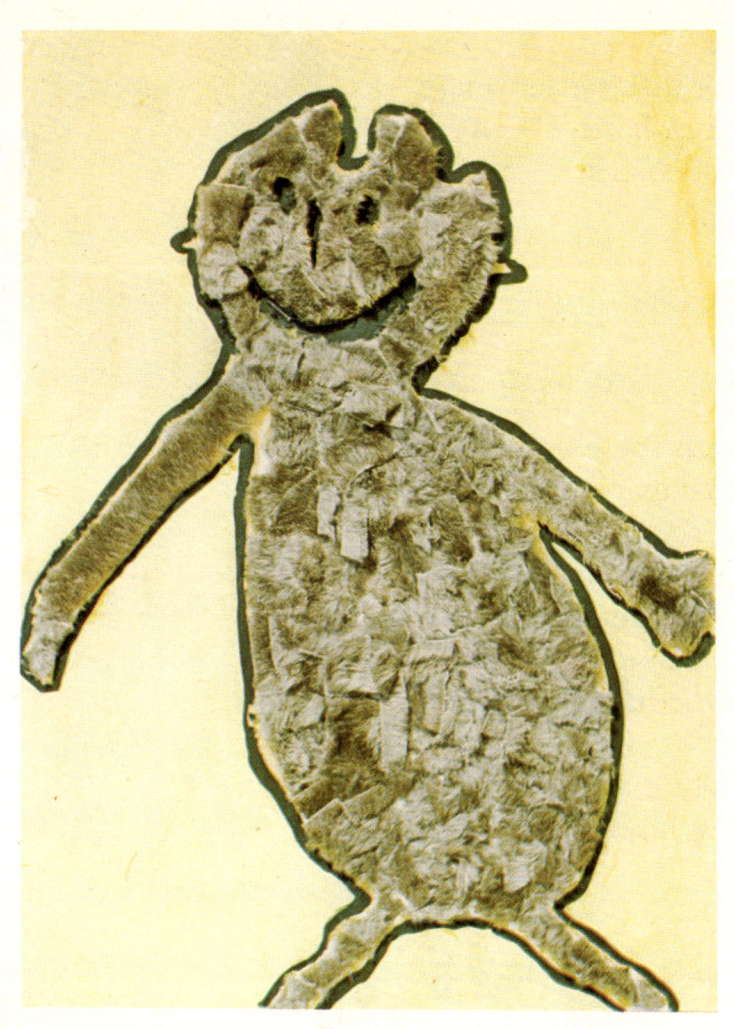

... made this splendid bear!

roller, or finish off your material picture by using crayon for the sky and grass, or just as sweeps of colour to unite your designs.

Pencil and charcoal sketching

Collect together
1. Black pencils of different strengths: H–hard, F–medium hard, B–soft black, 2B–very soft black
2. Coloured pencils
3. Charcoal
4. Crayons
5. White paper

How to start
1. Experiment with the black pencils, noticing which makes your sketching and shading easier.
2. Choose a subject around your home or school and sketch it, either as a rough copy to be made in detail later, or as an immediate finished sketch.
3. Use charcoal alone for some of your drawings, noticing how soft it is and how easily it rubs.

Now experiment
It is useful to have a rough notebook in which to make pencil sketches and then to experiment by using different kinds of materials for rough and good copies.

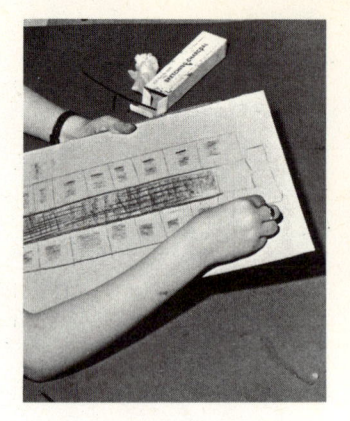

Charcoal is soft to use . . .

. . . and looks well combined with pencil for sketching.

Pile up chairs together and then sketch them from a distance, or make a drawing of the view from your window. Remember you can use many different materials in one picture to bring out light, colour and detail.

Put together a group of objects, or people, and sketch them. You may need to experiment by making a number of drawings from different angles, using different papers and colours.

Egg box pictures

Collect together
1. Some empty cardboard egg boxes
2. Strong glue such as Copydex (P.V.A. glue is good for this and can be bought in small tubes.)
3. Brush
4. Thickly mixed powder paint
5. Large sheet of card
6. Scissors

How to start
1. Draw your outline on the card.
2. Fill in the design with the egg box pieces, gluing them on one side and fitting them closely together. Cut them into one or two sections if necessary.
3. Press the boxes firmly together and firmly down on to the card.
4. When completed, paint your design and add a thickly painted outline.

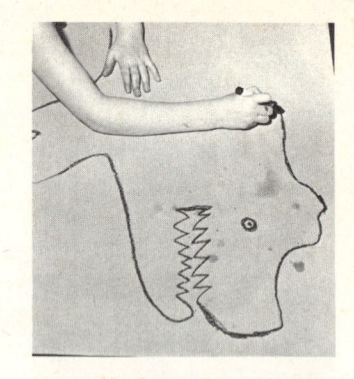

Egg boxes are ideal for large pictures.

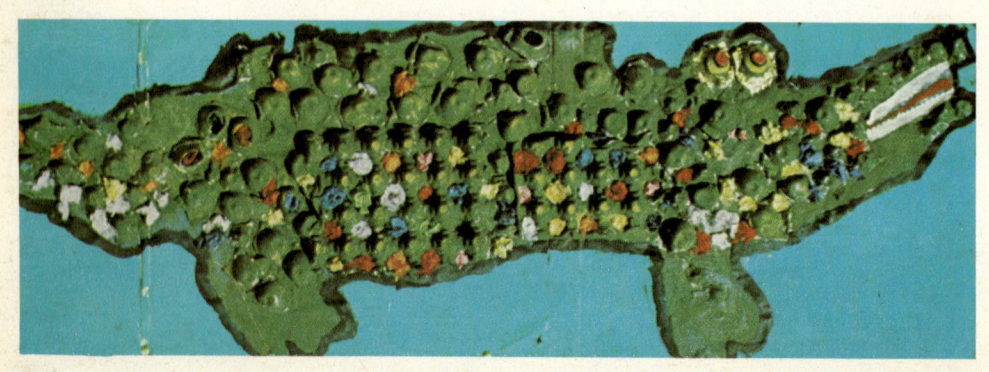